Long Live The Queens

C J Excellence

PREFACE

This book is inspired by and dedicated to all the amazing women in the world that have influenced me. The Nina Simones to the Regina Kings and some of my favorite teachers growing up like Ms. Turner, Mrs. Nelson, and Ms. Houston. From artists like Sue Tsai to entrepreneurs like Ming Lee that bring beauty to life through their work, granting us access to just a glimpse of their world via social media. To the activists that we may not know by name but their contributions make the world a better place to live in. To the women in my family: Georgie, Jennifer, Karmon, and Kim—who have always pushed me to be my best. I recall listening to stories about men in their lives that never lived up to their promises. I knew at an early age that I never wanted to grow up and be viewed as a broken promise. Their stories inspired me to be the idea of what I feel a great man should be: a great listener, compassionate, understanding, loving, empathetic, loyal, honest, trustworthy, and reliable.

My Grandmother "Shirley Troutman" (my dad's mom) is the most beautiful person inside and out that I may ever know. Your positive view on life, soft voice, and loving heart make me even more appreciative to have someone as amazing as you in my life. To my aunts Teresa (Bone), Debbie, Paula, and Carolyn: Thank you for your love and endless support. To my cousins: My life has been better because of you all. I am forever grateful.

To the woman whom I have loved and will always love, "Dee": You have taught me so much and we have created so many invaluable memories together. Thank you for loving me and always giving your best in all that you do. I appreciate you beyond words.

If you are not mentioned by name, I want you to know how special you are to me. I couldn't have written any of this without your influence. Every word in this book was written from a place of love, peace, and appreciation. This is one of the most important books I will ever write. Without any further delay, I bring to you *Long Live The Queens*.

CONTENTS

CHAPTER 1

Her Worth

Invaluable

She was a breath of fresh air
in a world that lacked oxygen,
built with the anatomy to bring life
while blessed with the ability to remain breathtaking.
How could anyone neglect
the amazing attributes that she embodied?
Redefining the idea of royalty,
remaining forever priceless to me.

Incomparable

You could live three lifetimes
and never meet anyone who was comparable to her.
She had a unique quality about her
that at times seemed hard to put into words,
but that couldn't stop you from recognizing her worth.
The qualities of brilliance that naturally lived within her
influenced you to always have her back.
'Cause the connection you had with one another was
simply unmatched.

So Much About Her

She was the embodiment of everything fine.
Not just based off of her physical features,
but the kindness she shared with others,
and how she carried herself said so much about her.
To her nieces and nephews,
she was their favorite aunt.

If she had children, she was the first person
they'd speak of while accepting an award.
"I'd like to thank my mom for always instilling in me
that I can accomplish anything I put my mind to
and assuring me of my excellent capabilities within my
lifetime.
You are my support system, my guidance, and my
strength. I love you, mom."

Her Ingredients

If Queens could be built,
the ingredients would consist of her.
She was that type of a woman;
She was built with a
mind of brilliance,
heart of gold
and attitude that inspired you to be
the best you could possibly be.

Her Love

You couldn't put a price tag on her love;
She was eternally priceless.
Her integrity couldn't be compromised;
She was a one-of-a-kind painting
that could never be placed on auction.
You valued her like a heartbeat,
effortlessly adding more color and flair to your soul.

Her Importance

Life without her would be hard to imagine.

She was such an intricate part of the fabric of your reality.

You appreciated her like Pac appreciated Afeni.

Her presence seemed as important as life itself.

Queen of Ambition

The narrowly marketed images of beauty
couldn't equate to the woman you knew her to be.
She strived to be more than people expected.
She was in tune with herself,
knowing that her potential was limitless.

She was the Queen of Ambition
living on a throne
where commendable royalty is often found,
mentally rooted in her purpose
and forever deserving of her crown.

Something About Her

She made lemonade from freshly picked lemons
and the best pies and cakes you'd ever desire to taste.
She was Lois Lane with the qualities of Wonder Woman,
turning nothing into something from scratch.
It was just something about her that was simply
unmatched.

Gifted

Beauty lived within her complexity;
It was a part of her genius.
Evolving at her own pace,
redefining what a "queen" is,
turning losses into lessons,
transforming purpose from pain.

Even with odds stacked against her,
she managed to gain.
She was magic without the magician costume
who was gifted beyond measure.
She was the one without question,
now and forever.

Valued

Seeing her as royalty was not that hard of a task.
She was remarkably generous,
even sacrificing her last.
She was spiritually wealthy
so material things didn't mean much.
It's not that she didn't enjoy the finer things,
she just valued
time,
respect,
integrity,
and loyalty.

Even when she didn't have it all figured out,
she still did her thing.
To know her is a blessing.
She is Earth's most gracious human being.

Simple Math

Through experience,
she learned that when things didn't add up,
she should never subtract herself.
If she received an offer that didn't reflect her value,
she negotiated her worth.

Regardless of the brand of her purse
or the designer of her heels,
she remained authentic to her truth.
Forever unapologetically real,
she demanded respect without request,
validated her purchases with receipts,
and focused on a successful life of great
health, wealth, and increase.

She learned that receiving your value can be war.
But by the time they realized her worth,
she was worth more.

Transformation

They saw her growth
and mistakenly dismissed it as mere change,
failing to realize that once a caterpillar becomes a butterfly,
they're never quite the same.

She turned ignorance into excellence.
Creativity was her expertise.
When funds were at their lowest,
she found ways to make them multiply and increase.
She weathered the storms,
not unscathed but wiser than before.
And for that, I love her
now and forevermore.

Her Strength

She unselfishly lived for an audience of one,
understanding that the best welfare is self-care.
Her actions spoke on maximum volume.
No one had her like she had herself,
often looking in the mirror if she needed help.

Then she realized the words from coaches, mentors, and
influential poets,
adding more octane to her engine of heroics,
living more fully without unwarranted stress,
and carrying the crown at her best.

Irreplaceable

It seemed like she was the only one for me
in this world.
In my world,
she was my everything.

Writing to You

She was unforced perfection,
even within her flaws.
Maybe she wasn't right for everyone,
but for me, she had it all.

She was often told that she was not enough
and a number of other lies
both directly and indirectly.
But those opinions were not sufficient.
She was enough
without the need of added ingredients.

I've tried to put it into words.
so I hope that she's reading this.
Her respect was due
like bills on the first.
It should never be neglected;
The priceless value of her worth.

CHAPTER 2

Poetically Just Us

P.J.U.

Together, we live as if we are stars in a motion picture.
Many scenes have been filmed with us apart,
but now that we're here
together,
we get to live the best part.

If Beale Street could talk,
it would say: "I love you like Fonnie loves Tish."
Even when physically incarcerated,
concrete walls couldn't confine our bliss.

A heavenly match made on earth.
A solid foundation built on organic loyalty and trust.
Visions of loving you forever.
Poetically just us.

Many Reasons

Life seems more amazing with you in it.

You give me a reason to keep going,

even at times when I feel like completely giving up.

You removing D, one E, and the letter I from the word depression,

gives me the strength to PRESS ON.

One of the many reasons why I love you:

You encourage me to carry on.

With Your Permission

I just want to bring you happiness
and remove your worries
I want to untether you from all
negativity,
past disappointments,
and blindsided betrayals.

You deserve better.
Better than before.
May my actions prove that my words are real
now and forevermore.

My Presence

At times, I don't say much.
I would prefer to under-promise and over-deliver,
making up for every empty promise you ever received
from anyone in this world
and for every time your hopes were up
only to later be let down.
I just want to bring you joy
every moment that I'm around.

Love Connection

How could Lucky know that he'd find Justice
on a seemingly regular day?

Regardless of your service provider,
nothing can kill love's connection
when it's meant for the long-term—
longer than 30-year mortgage terms,
longer than payments for student loans.

When we work together,
all parties benefit.
Like childhood games of tag,
together, we're it.

Black Mirror

What if the world was built for the two of us?
One giant simulation
created with the sole purpose of us finding each other
and growing to love one another
as we get to know each other.
Beautiful works of art
unconfined by a canvas frame,
taking occasional vacations and being transported by
plane.
'Cause when we're together, everything feels right
when experiencing this wonderful gift called life.

For You

Allow me to lead
and show you everything love should be.
There are very few forces in the world
that can compare to the bond of we.
Not ambiguous about my intentions,
I want to share my ambitions
and make sure that in every avenue of my life,
I provide a space that you belong in.

Beyond the Holiday

It doesn't have to be February 14th
for us to treat each other special.
I want to give you that feeling
like every day is your birthday
and like you're the center of attention,
an artistic centerpiece
with invaluable value
treated and respected as such,
with the sole purpose of letting you know
you mean so much.

Your Impact

I just want to get wealthy
and wake up to you.
Tony! Toni! Toné! vibes…
Just me and you.

I want a chemistry that could only be created by two.
I've thought of you my entire life
before I even knew your name.
Now that you're here
elevating my life,
nothing has been the same.

Keeping Us at Peace

Even when it seems like
we have nothing in this world,
we can sleep at night knowing
we have each other:
Partners in life.

Feeling better with you next to me…
Us against the world.
We are a part of each other's legacy.

Our Victories

I see more power in *we* than *I*.
You had me at "I got you."
I assured you that "I got us."

Dependability maintained our balance.
Loyalty,
Commitment,
Communication,
Honesty,
Love,
and understanding built our trust.

We're our own version of Queen & Slim
with a more beautiful ending.
We put past worries behind us
as we focus on continuously winning.

This

A different kind of intimacy:
Understanding each other's minds,
a connection that money cannot buy
and an understanding that goes beyond verbal cues.

Instead of making excuses,
together, we make moves.
Poetically just
in our approach to caring for one another.
A friendship at its core.
An award-winning motion picture
composed with the perfect score
is the only way to describe you:
the one whom I truly love and adore.

The ART of US

As we work to build our legacies,
the effort we put in isn't easy.
Sometimes, we might disagree.
Occasionally, we even fuss.
But at the end of the day,
it's all for the betterment of us.

Small brush strokes forming a bigger picture.
Individual bricks laid
building toward something bigger.
Creating a path for our future.
Increasing monetary figures.
Regardless of our financial gains,
together, we're richer.

True Balance

We turn hardships into great accomplishments.
Who has us like we have each other?
Together, we survive through turbulent storms.
Regardless of the forecasted weather,
we value each other's time
while nurturing each other's minds.
We build each other up
while remaining aligned.

That Feeling

"What's the secret to our longevity?"
they often ask.

We wake up each day and continue
to choose each other
each morning,
every night,
each hardship,
every fight.

We pick each other daily
because being together feels right.

CHAPTER 3

Moments & Memories

Time with You

Normal days become monumental memories;
Thinking back on days when it was just we.
Memories play back
like snapshots of favorite movie scenes.
Thinking of you—
only you
triumphant in life's boxing ring.

You're the air to my lungs,
the cure to my numbness.
Life is a temporary journey
but I choose to run with you,
only you—
hoping that we last forever.
I know all is well
as long as we're together.

Beloved

She reminded me of every word Jhené sang.
"While We're Young" played
mildly in the background.
Our connection and vibe was so majestic.

Directors,
actors,
actresses,
screenplay writers,
and an entire filming crew
could work tirelessly to capture
one of those cinematic moments
that remain ingrained in culture
captured on the big screen,
but we were the real thing.

Our daily lives were our own movie sets,
creating invaluable memories
we couldn't easily forget
and a love that could never be duplicated:
Authentic and factual.
Belonging together,
effortlessly natural.

Pure Greatness

Reminiscent of the Toni Braxton love song,
she means the world to me.
Even while apart,
separated by the enchanting faces
of a thousand beautiful blue ocean seas,
nothing... I mean nothing
could separate her love from me.

If I was incarcerated,
she would show up in the form of love letters.
She would effortlessly know
how to make me feel better
and say words to reignite our covenant.
She'd take my mind to places
where I relive the valuable time we spent.

I'd rather be in each other's arms
or in the mental vault of each other's minds.
Just as valuable as life itself;
The greatest of all time.

Thinking About You

A love like yours is an acquired taste:
Reflecting back on the day we first met,
never knowing where time would take us
and guided by intuitive steps.

Starting off as close friends
and gradually building an understanding
that led to an attraction.
Our connection then became richer—
The memories, everlasting.

Everyday

Time with you seems priceless.
If memories were for sale,
I'd buy more
just to properly archive our time together.

We are fans of each other
and a part of the same team.
I'm here to assist in straightening your crown
in the event that it ever leans.
You're admired for your poise, strength, and vision,
and make each moment in life worth living.

Moments Like These

Each moment with you seems purposeful,
as if I'm exactly where I'm supposed to be.
I walk in the direction
of my own fate
to meet up with destiny.
We dance in sync to the rhythm and beat
with perfect precision.
It's a dance with destiny
I never thought I'd envision.

Something Special

I can recall the very first time
I had to go:
I was just about to walk out of the door
and then the phone started to ring.
You walked over to answer it.
As you took the call,
you looked back
and gazed directly in my eyes
while you gently said:
"I Love You."

Sharing Our Thoughts

Her: Why do you love me?

Him: Because you make life an experience worth having.

Her: What are some of your favorite memories of us?

Him: Where do I begin...

Memories Part 1

Him: I remember the proms we attended.
During the first one,
your older cousin was our personal chauffeur,
driving us around for the night.

You arrived at my house dressed in blue;
That dress looked perfect on you.
Mom and Grandma took pictures of us
in the living room.
We dressed to impress like a bride and groom.

We had only known each other shortly:
A few months or so at most.
Who knew that from that seed of a first date,
a love would grow.

That night, I met your sister Tee Tee.
How could I know in that moment
that I'd be meeting our kids' future auntie.

We took a picture as a couple,
then one as a group.
We socialized a little bit
and shortly after, we split.

Memories Part 1.5

Him: We went further to the other side
of the connected venues.
My school prom was held that same day.
We didn't have a ticket but we went anyway.
My school prom was like an unofficial concert
so we decided to stay.

I look back on this now,
realizing that this was our first official date.
And even though it has been many years
since that night came to pass,
I appreciate each moment we shared
as if it were our last.

Memories Part 2

Her: Do you have any other favorite memories?

Him: Being present when Jason was born,
watching him leave your body,
witnessing his first moment
that would lead to the story of his life…
Then you looked over and told me
"I love you."

Years later, watching Jada's birth,
holding your hand during the C-section,
anticipating the arrival of the daughter
we had imagined and talked about for years
become a part of our reality
and texting Jason a picture of her
as he anxiously waited in the waiting area
with the rest of the family
for his one and only sibling.
You were beyond happy;
We finally had the daughter we dreamed of.

Memories Part 2.5

Him: The vacations:
Las Vegas
Denver
Jamaica
New York
Myrtle Beach
Charlotte
Pensacola beach
Birmingham
Savanna
Tybee Island
New Jersey
Virginia
Gatlinburg/Pigeon Forge
Nashville.

Moving to metro Atlanta from Ohio
because we both wanted a change.
Deciding Georgia was for us
and would be the perfect place.

It seems that time flies at a pace hard to describe,
but I will forever hold onto
the memories of our lives.

Memories Part 3

Her: One last question. Do you feel that I have changed you?

Him: Without question.
We've spent more than half of our lives
being a part of each other's lives.
I wouldn't be a fraction of the person that I am now
if our lives never crossed paths.

The lows,
the highs,
the bright and dark times
are all a part of our story.
I wouldn't be who I am today without you.

CHAPTER 4

Imperfectly Perfect

The Rise of Queens

Like flowers that grow in the concrete jungle,
you would think many would marvel
at their excellence
instead of treating them as less than humble.

Could you imagine
how real their struggle must have been
when breaking through the confinement of concrete
in order for their lives to begin,
criticized for the way they looked
instead of marveling at their growth.

They kept an optimistic mindset
inspired by hope.
They lived with rich stories—
stories that captured the time they spent
overcoming seemingly impossible odds
and rising above their environment.

Better Understanding

You weren't blind
to the challenges she faced.
Whether they were internal or external,
you loved her the same—
for more than her worst mistakes
or any unflattering traits.
They didn't make her less beautiful
or less deserving of grace.

So you worked to understand her.
Oftentimes by just listening.
It wasn't a forgotten art
and as you got to know her,
she won your heart.

Day Brighter

She was liked because of her fearless qualities,
but she was loved despite her flaws.
Imperfectly perfect,
but embraced through it all.
You loved her while she was with you
and missed her while she was away.
Any time spent with her
elevated your day.

Her Own Rules

Many misconceptions
and mislabeled labels of perfection
didn't fit her.
They made her think that she shouldn't dream
so she dreamed bigger.
They thought that she would live her life in poverty
so she got richer.
Regardless of her background, she found a way.
That's why so many people admire her style
to this day.

Magic

Beautifully complex,
beautiful complexion.
She didn't have to fit your idea of perfection
in or out of context.
She had that magic,
turning ordinary things into instant classics.
She had a mind that rivaled Einstein's
in her own poetic way.
She created a legacy that transformed lives
that flowed through the bloodline of her DNA.

She had a past that only made her stronger
for her future and present
with a heart made of armor
for all the times she was tried
or severely neglected.
She stayed ready for life's exam
'cause she was not to be tested.

Golden Roots

Criticized for her natural hair
that grew naturally from her scalp—
as if it weren't designed to reach for the sun
or beyond the atmosphere of earth's house.
It was soft, dark, and beautiful.
Many people admired
and even attempted to touch
one of her many gifts
that some wanted to clutch.

Instead, it grew silky long,
tangled and short
or soft as the fuzz on a Georgia peach.
Her hair was her hair
no matter who put her down.
Her hair was her hair
fit for her crown.

Beyond Valuable

She may not have checked all of the boxes
due to societal conditioning
of what she should look like
by height, trim, or shade,
how flat her stomach should be,
or how bubbly her personality could be,
but despite anyone's discomfort of her merely being,
she found her wealth in remaining herself,
looking in the mirror if she needed any help
and figuring things out
by relying on her strengths.
Despite society's opinion of her packaging,
she was a gift.

Ignorance to Flames

They threw gasoline at her self-esteem
and attempted to drown her.
But little did they know,
she was already fire.

Higher Vibration

She validated her future,
learned priceless lessons from her past,
and wouldn't give the people that betrayed her
the time of day to kiss her ass.

She was fierce
and she was real.

She was the best version of herself:
a true queen of ambition
with a mindset of wealth.

Maya

Look at where she came from,
look at what she went through.
If it was you,
you'd have no other choice
but to be strong too.

She endured the uncomfortable
and pursued the seemingly impossible.
She was the once caged bird that had the audacity to sing,
never bounded by imperfections
and consistently flourishing.

Holding onto Triumph

Maybe while growing up
enough people didn't have her best interests.
Maybe they were more interested
in what they could get from her
both physically and financially
instead of pouring into her
and being the medicine she needed.

A lack of compassion can impact
one's perceived personal potential.
It can breed insecurities
and mess with your mental state.
Self-worth wasn't taught early on
so she had to develop it
on her own.

She had been through some things
that reshaped her
but didn't make her less desirable—
not to her core friends that would die for her,
those few people in life
that made it even more worth living.

To know her is to love her more.

The start of her journey

wouldn't be the final chapter,

overcoming her roughest days

that seemed like beautiful disasters.

CHAPTER 5

Blue Moon

Blue Moon

A byproduct that sometimes comes with love
and a side effect of its medicine:
those heartbreaks and aches
that don't get mentioned
towards the end of its commercial.
The things not often expressed:
when love has seemingly knocked out your heart,
draining you from feeling full
and tearing a piece of you apart.

A form of social distancing
minus the pandemic.
It happens in a rush
'cause all I want is you,
but I guess wanting you wasn't enough…

The Change

We used to be close.

Together, we brought light into a room.

Now I recently found out

that you live on the moon.

We're giving each other outer space.

Far from close as we once were.

Distance creates differences

and past times become a blur.

Lately

Learning to live without you
would be a reality I wouldn't want to face.
Your smile,
your fragrance,
all the way down to your taste.

How did we get here?
We've been going through a tough time lately.
We just haven't been the same.
I guess even with beautiful acres,
you'll come across a rough plain.

I'm not quite sure how long they last.
Anything worth working on
can't be bogus.
I'm taking an inventory of our journey,
and I miss the old us.

Wanted Forever

Now that you're gone,
should I come to this conclusion?
The reality that we had
was a beautiful illusion.
Maybe it was destiny
to not beautifully coexist.
I always wanted forever,
but how did it come to this?

Better Times

What happened to the
palm trees,
beach views,
restaurant dates,
ordering red velvet waffles & wings
or anything we wanted on the menu?
I'd cover the bill
but sometimes you'd try to pay anyway.
We had so many good times,
but now we're in a different place.

Giving Your Word

Promise no promises that can't be kept.
Take diligent action with each step
toward what you said you were going to do.
You volunteered, in fact,
without any pressure put on you
or any strings attached.
So what happened
to the things you were talking about?
The little trust that I did have
has now been clouded by doubt.

Starting a new chapter,
expecting more,
and settling for less
because promises are pointless
if they are not kept.

When Queens Recognize

I thought you were the one,
but my good heart let me down
'cause over time, I found out that you're a clown.
Of course, I didn't see the face paint,
but I clearly could see the signs,
indicating your intention
for what you had in mind.

But I'd rather stay where I'm at
than deal with you and your circus.
I hope you now know that I'm forever done;
You serve me no purpose.

Someone else may enjoy your performance,
but I won't be around.
My time is far too precious
to entertain a soulless clown.

Ignored Signs

I knew you'd take so much out of me.
Specializing in phlebotomy,
I should have seen the signs,
but love made me blind.
I gave and I gave,
and what did I get back in return?
A slightly broken heart
with a vault of lessons learned.

Landscaping

When you plant your love
in a toxic heart
that doesn't have any contact with sun,
you shouldn't be surprised over time
by the inevitable outcome.

Their Actions

It's heartbreaking
when you're willing
to go to the moon and back for someone
who's not even willing to stand up for you.
The silence can speak volumes.
The act of inaction can be deafening.

When promises become empty,
things become clearer.
It's not me,
it's the reflection that you see in the mirror.

Nine to Five

Have you ever worked a job
and got passed up for a promotion
you know you're qualified for,
only to realize you've outgrown the place
and find a job that pays and values you more?

That's kind of what this feels like
when someone doesn't truly know
what they have with you,
only to realize it after they've lost you.
They kept you around for convenience,
but lost you over not seeing
your value.

Accountability

Right or wrong,
together, we are stronger.
Our connection isn't lost
and our love isn't gone.

Now I think of you
after hearing certain songs.
We've both been hurt
and we can work on
what went wrong.

To get through this,
we must close the distance,
so I apologize
for my part in this.

Loving with Patience

I can see the tire tracks on your heart,
and I wasn't the bus driver who put them there,
reversing back over you
and hoping that you'd perish in despair.

I know that past trauma
can have lasting effects,
and it's hard to start over…

I wish I could take the pain away
not only with my words and actions,
but by witnessing my patterns.
And I know it will take time for deep wounds to heal,
so I'll remain patient in the meantime
and cover the bus driver's bill.

Moonlight

Truly loving you is embracing forgiveness,
understanding shortcomings,
and making sure that we both have
each other's best interests.

I've experienced heartbreak,
and that doesn't make me love you any less.
I won't allow you to be impacted
by somebody else's B.S.

I'd rather be with bae,
I'd rather be with you.
I'm confident this will end,
bringing clarity to this blue moon.

CHAPTER 6

Love Wanted

Something Deemed Priceless

In an ever-changing society
where instant gratification seemed normalized,
she wanted something with timeless value,
something that's not often advertised,
something people could live multiple lifetimes
and still fail to achieve.

She wanted love in every aspect of her life:
unwavering love from her family,
undying love from her spouse,
passionate love for her career.

She didn't want the story of her life to read
like pointless episodes experienced without depth.
She wanted long term-happiness,
a life she could look back on…
Smiling,
joking,
laughing,
and at times crying as she'd reminisce.

She could see it as clear as the stars above:

Something deemed priceless,

the invaluable beauty of love.

Best of Love

They say that love is a losing game,
so why do we entertain it?
Like playing the lottery despite the odds,
we play with the hope to win.
We play and hope to never get fatigued,
hurt, angry, or unexpectedly feel alone.

We play because love is the best part of us;
the foundation of a happy home.
We're all human and make mistakes,
and no one person
wins the lottery of perfection.
We're just trying to find the best of love
without misguided direction.

Estimated Time of Arrival

She just wants someone who treats her right
and knows that she's special;
a consistent flow of love
that always arrives on schedule.

Big Picture

No longer settling for less,
seeking what was best for her.

In an age where most settled for snacks,
she preferred a meal.
Where most settled for a watered down version of love
and empty hook-ups,
she worked towards something real.

Oftentimes, she would get hurt.
But she didn't expect her path to be stainless.
Because she knew...
The pursuit of true love often isn't painless.

An Anonymous Message

Your phone is on silent;

It's under your pillow

and we're laying together...

I guess I wasn't supposed to notice—

Not this time.

Acting all strange can lead to trust issues,

but if I find out you're playing games,

I'll be the first thing that you lose.

Maybe we're not on the same page

or even in the same chapter...

You say that you love me,

but what are you really after?

Reminders

She worked on seeing through the lies.
You know, the ones people tell to get you,
then you later find out
they are somebody else
or somebody else's...

It's a constant reminder for you
to take care of yourself.

For Dear Life

Far too often,

we accept the roses and ignore the thorns.

We hold on despite the pain,

repeatedly accepting the excuses

instead of the truth

that can be seen so plainly.

Need for Love

Have you ever felt like
you weren't the favorite?
More tolerated than appreciated,
more of a default choice
than anybody's first pick.
Not the most desirable,
but they'll settle for it.
The last kid to be selected on the team
for some reason,
not the first choice of their dreams.

Little do they know…
You have the biggest heart of them all,
just yearning to be appreciated—
flaws and all.
You're loyal at all times without acting funny
and you'd go to the moon and back
and not ask for gas money.

It repeatedly plays in the studio of our minds:
the need for the feeling of genuine love
in this lifetime.

Absent

They claimed they wanted you,
but failed to take out the time
to truly value you.

I wish I could bring back
that hopeful aspect of happiness
that was once in your eyes
and turn your days
back to sunlight and blue skies.

I really miss the days
when love was still in your eyes.

Inner Strength

She told me something that affected her soul
and completely transformed the woman she was,
impacting her perspective on the beauty of love.
She unexpectedly found out
that the DNA of the man she knew to be her father
didn't match that of her own.

And like a match,
this one event ignited and sparked a fire of pain.
Her father chose to disown her
and never spoke to her again.
He had been with her since she took her
first steps in Brooklyn,
delivering a hard blow in life
that hit her while she wasn't looking.

She decided not to give her fiery pain
the oxygen it needed to breathe.
Even though things seemed grim,
she chose to move forward
and remained strong without him.

Fighting for Love

Heartbreak can be so devastating,
leading you to never want to love again.
You think about distancing yourself
from everyone
and become numb.

There's an absence of love and the presence of hurt
that leave you in a conflicted state.
Love didn't live up to its promise,
and you feel betrayed.

But dark days only get better
with the presence of light,
so you choose not give up on love
and continue to fight.

More Than Meets the Eye

We are human beings,
not machines.
We don't come programmed
with default buttons to turn off feelings.

We're all dealing with our own personal problems,
so we end up purchasing material things,
hoping to fill us up,
but still feel slightly empty inside.

We want to feel more appreciated,
more loved,
more alive,
but we're edited with filters on social media,
concealing the full picture of our lives.

The Truth Is...

All I ever wanted was your love,
a sign that you genuinely cared
and would actually be there.

I wanted to know that if I ever got sick,
you'd be my urgent care,
that even when things weren't looking good
you'd still be near.

I never needed to be drowned by love,
I just wanted to feel that it was real.
As days and situations change,
the truth is eventually revealed.

A Place Called Love

Their inability to love you the right way
started to show indirectly
in general conversations
that you saw as small imperfections,
like forgetting to give you even a small gift
on your birthday.

You chalked it up as the good
outweighing the bad.
You even painted their red flags white
and surrendered to love
despite their obvious flaws.

The promises they made
often seemed more empty.
The excuses seemed reasonable
and at times, even convincing.

Because after all of the frustration
and disappointment was washed away,
you were looking for a place called love,
and they honestly didn't know how to love you
the right way.

Deserved Love

When you have a big heart,
the lines of love and manipulation
can be blurred.
You have the best interest for others,
but that same energy
is not always reciprocated.

They're masked in a veil of deceit
and more intrigued by all that they can receive
when they're not even in the business
of loving you
in the way that you need.

You deserve a great lover,
not limiting their solicitude and respect for you.
You also deserve an appreciative receiver
who makes a conscious effort
to assist in everything that's best for you.

Self-Love

Using her magic to her advantage,
she made the best out of all situations.
Even when she was called "ugly",
she quietly whispered to the woman within...
"You Gotta Love Yourself."

She redefined the term
and lived by her own rules,
understanding that the best love
doesn't start once you leave the house,
it starts from within.

CHAPTER 7

She Had Vision

Continued Legacy

A visionary like Dr. Mattie Moss Clark,
an entrepreneur like Madam C.J. Walker,
a pioneer like Claudette Colvin,
and the poetic souls of
Dr. Maya Angelou and Nikki Giovanni
create history in all that they've done
while reshaping culture and our reality
as we know it.

Then we have you:
You're highly capable of anything you put your mind to.
You walk in the purpose of your legacy,
stand on the shoulders of giants,
and live life with dignity.

Natural Foresight

She was a student who eventually became the teacher
and was so influential.
She took me to aspirational heights
and she pushed me to graduate,
not in terms of formal education,
but she inspired me to graduate in multiple aspects of life.

She was light years ahead
and gifted with natural foresight,
but compassionate enough to reassure you
that everything would be alright.

She turned me onto new things—
Things that I grew to love.
And at the same time,
I grew to love her even more.

Her Story

Some knew her name,
but very few knew her story.
She had dreams of making it
out of generational poverty,
turning disappointments into direct deposits.
She created valuable and profitable things,
turning wasted energy from others
into invoices... Cha-Ching!

Her flooded hardships
didn't drown her. In fact,
she strategized to win at life
despite any systemic traps.

Rene

Counting her out
would only be a testimony to your lack of judgement.
She started her own business
when a job offered her mediocre pay.

"But Rene, this is what the job pays..."
Instead of allowing the company to write
the details of her future,
she made money stretch like elastic
and rise like yeast.

She was not to be taken advantage of.
She was centered in her own personal peace.

Clear Vision

Living with a benevolent heart,
things changed by the renewal of her mind.
She saw the world differently,
no longer blind.

The distinguishing quality that she had
was that she didn't quit
on the things that she loved,
on her own ideas
or on the path that she saw fit.

Queen Behavior

She was a voice for the voiceless,
keeping things intact
for the betterment of people
and she always had their back.

Forever Inspirational

She no longer lived in fear.
She only believed in restructuring her reality,
annihilating anything that could hinder her
from keeping her vision clear.

She made you want to do better for yourself,
not by asking
but by igniting a fire within you
that inspired a desire for more
so that you could live every dream
you could ever possibly ask for.

Golden Language

She spoke a golden language,
releasing riches with each word,
but didn't hesitate
to defend herself if needed.
She had been through too much,
seen too much,
overcame too much
to settle for anything less than admiration.
She spoke life into the world
without any hesitation.

She realized that destructive talk
only became destructive towards herself.
So instead of using words like wrecking balls
and causing destruction to her life,
her words became more like cranes,
building to make a better life
and forever increasing her gains.

Not Boxed In

She diligently thought differently.
Any walls that were built to confine her,
she thought of ways to destroy
or overcome them.
If she was taught to be poor,
she'd strategize on building wealth.
If she was taught to be reliant,
she thought of more ways to be self-sufficient.

Honestly, she didn't have everything figured out
and that was okay.
Because if something didn't sit right with her
and she desired to change it,
she found a way.

Moving On

Deciding that drama was too expensive
of a dysfunctional place to rent,
she retired from playing games
and was completely over it.

Return on Investment

Dreaming without limits
and building from her imagination.
She invested in properties,
living a real-life monopoly.
She had visions of being on boards
and being a shareholder,
increasing her cash flow
as her business began grow.

Even at times
when the reality of her dreams
didn't seem closer,
she maximized her investment,
allowing good karma to flow over.

Different

She dedicated her life to do you right,
loving deeply and honestly
and hoping that level of love would be reciprocated.
But as a queen, she recognized
that not everyone is gonna appreciate
the sacred nature of pure love—
Not like her.

She was exquisite gourmet
in a society obsessed with fast food.
She was fluent in class,
so there was no need to be schooled.

Her Wisdom

She taught me about real strength.

It's not measured by how you flex your muscles.

Instead, it's measured by how you flex your mind.

She had unmatched vision
and was forever ahead of her time.

Golden Crowns

She was a part of a group of friends—
more like sisters—
who collectively thought amongst themselves:
If not us,
then who?
If we're not gonna take our dreams seriously now,
then when?

The answers were always overwhelmingly
Us and *Now.*
So they kept that energy around themselves
and turned obstacles into opportunities
amongst many other things.
They were bonded beyond measure,
a true team of queens.

Sister Circle

They didn't just run together,

they pushed one another,

assuring that each one got closer to their goal—

whatever that goal may have been.

They had "What About Your Friends" by TLC vibes.

Not only were they close friends,

they were an essential part of each other's lives.

Wealth Mindset

She specialized in coming through in the clutch
like a game-winning play
on a dwindling clock,
seeing pathways
where others could only see roadblocks.

She knew how to get the job done.
Regardless of the odds,
she made a way out of no way
because giving up wasn't a valid response.

Dreams into Reality

She elevated her family
by reshaping her family tree
and creating brilliant branches,
ultimately leading to a dynasty.

Whether she received the credit or praise,
the truth still remains the same:
She had vision,
so we honor her name,
even in Family Matters.

She never kept her wins low,
investing in herself
then watching her dividends grow.

She never had a six-figure family member
until she became one.
And since she did things right,
her good deeds couldn't be undone.

CHAPTER 8

November

Dear November,

I refer to you as the month of appreciation.
So allow me to give thanks
to those who deserve recognition
but far too often, don't receive it
as much as they should.

My beautiful days would not shine so bright
without you in my life.
Those who remain amazing
deserve the most gratitude.
So without further ado…
This is for you.

Truly Appreciated

Allow me to give you roses;
You deserve them.

So many people are genuinely loved,
but we don't tell them.

So I just wanna give you flowers
while you can still smell them.

We can all pause and show our appreciation,
even when life seems overwhelming.

You deserve all of the admiration in the world,
and that goes without question.

Admiring You

Thank you for existing, Jada.
I was so inspired by you as a child.
My daughter now shares the same name.
I gave it new meaning for the person Dee and I created.
Jason and Danielle's Addition…

Your star power has shined bright for decades.
And the energy that you've shared on earth
will continue to positively affect lives for centuries to come.

You called out the Oscars for lack of diversity
at a time when extremely brilliant artists were being
overlooked and undervalued.
It was not popular to speak out,
but you felt it was right,
and it speaks to the character of the amazing person you
are.

As a result of your actions,
once blinded eyes have now acknowledged
groundbreaking work.

Long Live The Queens

You've opened more eyes to the importance of Table
Talks with honest expression.
Therapeutic in many ways,
gradually reducing the size of the stigma.

I thank you for the drops that you've added to the pool of
humanity.
Drops that have created a ripple effect in the water of
culture.
Thanks for all that you do,
no matter how big or small it may seem.
You're imperfectly perfect,
an Amazing Queen.

A Trotwood Gift

I can remember
you sitting in the front of the class,
calmly explaining how you fought
for a course that reflected history
of people that looked like you and me...

They say you don't know where you're going

until you understand where you've been.
In each person's life experiences
lie many lessons.

You taught us that we come from a resilient culture,
continuously striving and surviving
despite discrimination and vultures.
You showed us documentaries like "Eyes on The Prize"
and created a curriculum that not only nurtured our minds,
but gave us identity and purpose,
allowing us to know that in adversity, we rise.
And because of you, I'm more prideful
of who I am.
So the least I could do is show my appreciation
in this poem:

Thank you, Ms. Houston!

Thankful for You

I just read online
about two good childhood friends of mine.
Their mother was involved in a serious car accident.
It really caught me off guard,
so allow me to vent...

I read she had two injuries
and was taken to the hospital
for immediate surgery.
I scrolled further to read
that the surgery went fine and she'll be okay,
but the person in the other car actually passed away.

Life happens so fast.
I haven't seen her in years...
I do remember how caring and kind she is.
It made me think about
how she used to listen our songs and raps
in the basement
and bring us both breakfast
the morning after a sleepover.

Long Live The Queens

She'd drive us to the studio

or any place we needed to go

in her black Kia SUV.

I wasn't her child,

but she always made me feel like family.

It's nothing comparable to the love of a mother,

so I pray for her healing as she recovers.

Thank you!

April 2020

My aunt Debbie once said:

"God won't let this many prayers go unanswered"

as my dad laid in ICU

being assisted by a ventilator

after testing positive for Covid-19.

I'll forever hold on to what you said…

Because of your words,

I knew he had a fighting chance to live.

I just want you to know

how beautiful of a gift that was to give.

Love you, Aunt Deb!

Loving Us

Let's get the family together
for more things than funerals.
Let's replace tears from mourning
with tears of joy.

Let's celebrate life!
This life
that we've each been gifted.

Sharing similar DNA,
we've been through some rough times
but ultimately, we've made a way.

Let's utilize our time.
Let's make things right.
'Cause there's no family like family
morning, noon, or night.

Family Tree

Four generations connected by genetic code,
traveling this life path
on separate roads:
Georgetta,
Georgie,
Jennifer,
Jada...
My sheroes without capes,
allowing this adventure called life
to be a more tolerable place.

I wouldn't be anywhere near
The man that I am
without your sacrifice and grace.

For you all,
I give my all.
Purely rooted in love,
I cherish you all dearly
and place nothing above.

Georgetta

I never got the pleasure to meet you;
Our lives exist on different timelines.
Even though we never got to talk to or greet each other,
your life still has an impact on mine.

I still hear stories of your pure spirit:
naturally caring and empathetic.
I can recall visiting the place
where you and your twin sister are laid to rest.

You've had such a profound effect on me.
Due to the seeds of love you planted
in your daughter Georgie,
her influence has changed me.

I thank you for that.
Even though we never got to spend time together or even a
day, it's ironic how things play out that way.
I just want you to know
and I feel I need to say
that I love and appreciate you always.

Sincerely,
CJ

P.S. Love you, great grandma!

Georgie

I'm listening to my grandma hum
"What a Wonderful World"
and thinking about how wonderful of a person she's been
to me.

You worked for Inland/General Motors
for 30 years with the weight of raising four kids on your
shoulders.
You fought for your fair slice of the American pie,
knowing that genuine efforts pay off in due time—
Years after you bought your house
in the suburbs with a pool,
even after you used my bib to wipe my baby drool.

You taught me the importance of managing my finances
and paying my bills early and on time
back when people wrote checks
and before mobile billing online.

You taught me that on the road of life
not all things come easy
and many people

Long Live The Queens

don't believe fat meat is greasy.

They lack common sense,

but you add to my common sense.

And I can still feel Georgetta's love

radiantly beaming through your presence.

Georgie Continued

More than a grandmother,

I always want to be more like you:

giving,

forgiving,

hard-working

and honest.

If God gave favorable guarantees,

you are his promise.

The universe is a more special place

because of your love.

And I cherish every moment we've had

down to the warmth of your hug.

Thank you, grandma!

Jennifer

She had her first child at age 18
and a second son shortly after her 20th birthday.
She was a teenage mother trying to raise Boys to Men
while striving to figure out her own life
and working to transform two princes into kings.

How could she defy the odds
with those odds stacked against her?
She opened the oven on early mornings,
bringing heat to cold winters.
She attended baseball and basketball games.
From parent teacher conferences to helping with
homework.
She took her kids on trips
and enrolled them in programs to broaden their
perspective.
She prayed for them to live their best life possible
away from harm's way
completely protected.

As she got older,
she put more of her aspirational dreams.

on the backburner.

Nothing that she has done has gone unnoticed.

There are far too many things to mention on one page.

She is forever loved and appreciated.

and as priceless as they come.

I always want you to know

how much I love you, mom.

Thank you!

Jada

Some nights
I read poetry to my daughter
and as she sleeps peacefully.
I wonder about how things will be
once she gets older.
Will she find purpose and peace
in writing like I do?
I would be so proud to read the thoughts on her mind
expressed through written words.

I hope that she's proud of me.
I hope that she reaps all of the joys in life.
I hope that she knows how much she's appreciated and
loved.

And I'll support her decisions,
whatever she envisions.
Now to infinity…

Love you, Jada (a.k.a. Rosie)!

Best Interests

Now I can edify each queen
and speak on all of the brilliant things they do,
but all the roads in my life still lead back to you.
Dreams of loving you will never end.
I hope that you always remember
that I'll have your best interests.
I'm thankful for you like November.

CHAPTER 9

Years with You

Dawn

They took their first trip
together at Clearwater Beach
amongst warm sunrays,
beautiful blue water
and sand under their feet.

You'll never know how great life will be
until you start to live it.
And that, they did
with very few limits.

They returned ten years later
as a family of four,
having spent years together
loving one another even more.

If "this could be us" was a couple,
it would be them:
A valuable relationship,
a truly treasured gem.

Waking Up

I want...
I really want
loving you to be a part of my daily routine.
I don't open up to many people,

but I see something in you.
Despite my nervousness,
you seem irresistible.

I'd like to get to know you

and continuously build with you.
Hard to shake this feeling
I get at the thought of you.
I feel like a complete wreck without you;
I don't feel like myself.

Nearly eight billion people on this planet,
and I want you and no one else.
Time without you is unbearable;
Moments feel like weeks.
'Cause you bring me balance,
through life's uncertain lows and peaks.

Dreams Come True

She was a dream come true in physical form,
a once-in-a-lifetime encounter,
beyond the norm.

You'd thank God for the breath you took the day you both
met.
Instead, you remain grateful you crossed paths
without an ounce of regret.
But you both grew to appreciate one another over time.
In knowing her, you knew you found your person—
one of a kind.

Her presence brought purpose.
Her existence brought hope.
Infatuated with her potency,
she was that dope.

Thinking About Forever

Time spent with her was like vacationing from the world.
Words can barely describe what that feels like…
Curing my social anxiety
with the mere thought of her strength
and all the attributes that consist of her gifts:
a genius at heart,
genuine and kind,
bringing beautifully enhanced colors
to this dull life of mine.

Each day brings new gambles,
but everything about you feels right.
I wanna share each moment with you
for the rest of my life.

Marathons

Long-term relationships are not sprints.

They're more like marathons

ran together as one

with a common goal,

using past experiences to hydrate

one another in life's race,

maintaining a united pace,

building together,

and making things right

while remaining intact.

Celebrating anniversaries is like taking victory laps.

?

Have you ever had
an incomparable type of love
that was breathtaking at times
but always knew just how to bring you
right back to life?

Consistent for You

Flowers placed in a glass vase,
a heartfelt card with a signature at the bottom,
a personal letter and money enclosed
on special days or random days
just to show that I care.

And as long as I have breath,
I will always be there.

Seeing Your Growth

I'm in love with the woman you're becoming.
From the person you once were
to the incredible person you are today,
I am thankful to know you
and I appreciate you more each day.

The Love is Real

I don't want you for a phase,
I want you forever.
I often wonder what a future looks like
with us being together.

Us against the world...
Nah, more like the world against us.
We complement each other
and we value our trust.

Loving you more with each waking day,
the feelings I have for you
refuse to go away.

What We Have

When the world is cold,
you bring me comfort like a warm glove.
The best time is time spent with you.
Kissing you is my favorite drug.

You once told me
that gravity has less of an effect
when you're around me

and you feel like you're floating
by the mere presence of me.

And I feel the same way,
never regretting what we have.
We work,
we play,
we love,
we laugh.

In Love with You

Unrequited love, no more.
We've got something special.
You told me you love me,
and I can tell you were speaking from your soul.

Your eyes light up in my presence.
You say I'm the best part of your day.
I want to form gates around this moment;
I want this to stay.

Finding Happiness

I find happiness in you.
The one thing people spend a lifetime searching for,
I've found in the one whom I adore.

The cure to my emptiness,
the perfect pass,
my completion…
I found that because of you,
and it changed my life.

Precious

This moment that we are living in,

this very moment,

right now,

the present—

It's the most precious gift we will ever have.

It helps form the future.

Its signature is the past.

I couldn't tell you what tomorrow holds,

but time is moving fast

and as long as we have each other,

I hope our love will forever last.

Full Circle

She said the thing she admires
the most about me is that
I turned out to be
the man I said I would be.

Born Gifted

If I thought about giving up a thousand times,
she gave me one million reasons to keep going.
That was her superpower.
And she may not be recognized
in the Marvel or DC universe,
but she made me realize one of many things:
my worth.

Sharing Our Thoughts Part 2

Her: There are plenty of fine women out here—
some even gorgeous.
I'll be honest with you CJ,

I don't know if I can fully trust you.

Him: There are more than 7.4 billion people in the world—
Thousands that I've met,

hundreds I've gotten to know,

dozens more personally,
but only a few had my best interests at heart.

Despite them all,
none of them can compare to you.
In a day filled with stress and confusion,
you bring me peace.
In a society obsessed with quantity,
you are the quality that fills me.
You are the perfectly produced track over lyrics that fit just
right.
And for that, I wanna share with you the most precious
thing I have, and that's my life.

Speaking from My Heart

Deep down inside,
you realize that I love you
more than you could ever ask for.
And it scares you to let your walls down
fully to your core.
Sometimes you may even ask yourself:
What does this man see in me
to make him feel that he wants to love me endlessly?
How could someone enter my life
willing to heal my wounds,
who adores my fragrance and occasionally buys me
perfume?

Together, we always seem to win—
a bond deeper than just friends,
someone who has my best interests at heart,
now until the end.

Special Thanks

I would like to give a special Thank You to everyone that made this book possible. It took four-and-a-half years of brainstorming and a lifetime of experiences to bring this poetic art to life. It truly means the world to me. Thanks to everyone who ever said a kind word, inspired, or disappointed me. I wouldn't have grown into the man I am today without you all. Lastly and most importantly, I'd like to thank you the reader for your time and support. If you enjoy this book, feel free to share it with anyone who may appreciate its contents.

From all aspects of my heart...
Thank you!

About The Author

CJ Excellence (also known as Clarence "Jason" McCullar) is an Ohio-raised, Georgia-residing writer. He started writing his first poems at six years old. At the age of 14, he wrote and recorded songs under the group name Teknical Elements. He has always had a passion for expressing himself through the art of writing. He has a strong love for family that is reflected in his work. Above all, CJ is a self-proclaimed "advocate for excellence" that he describes as being the best version of one's self.

Find him on Instagram: @CJExcellence

www.ingramcontent.com/pod-product-compliance
Lightning Source LLC
Chambersburg PA
CBHW070807100426
42742CB00012B/2276